LYNETTE'S LINEZ

IN THIS TOPZ ...

Hello! My name's Lynette, and I want to welcome you to this special issue of Topz Bible notes! If this is the first time you have read Topz and you're not sure what to do – the next page tells you all about it.

Becoming a Christian is the most important thing you could ever do in your life! If you're not quite sure about making that decision yet, these notes will help you. The first part is called 'All for you' and tells you all about what God has done for you, and how Jesus has made a way for you to become friends with God. Isn't that cool – God really wants to be your friend!

If you've already decided to become a Christian, still read this first part, as it will help you to understand more about the decision you've made. Then go on to the second section, which shows you how to grow closer to Jesus and get to know Him better. There's also a chance to read what some other children and some famous people think about being a Christian, and about the power of prayer.

I hope these notes help you to understand more about how much God loves you, how much He's already done for you – and how much more He's waiting to give you.

If you would like to receive Topz notes regularly – the last page will tell you how you can do that.

Right – get reading – and get to know God!

Love from

Lynette

Lynette Brooks (Topz Editor)

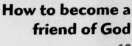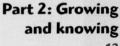

How to use Topz

It may be that some of you haven't looked inside a Bible very much before. If so, here's a few helpful hints:

1 Each day in Topz there's a Bible reading. It's shown like this:

Genesis 25 v 21–26

2 To find this, turn to the Contents page near the front of your Bible and look for the name of the book – which in the example above is Genesis.

Bible book

Page number

Contents

THE BOOKS OF THE OLD TESTAMENT

Now find the page this book starts on and turn to it.

3 You will have to turn on a few pages now to get to the right chapter.

4 Now look for the verse numbers which will be in smaller type. The chapter and verse will look like this:

Chapter number

Verse number

GENESIS 25

5 After reading the Bible passage, go back to the Topz page and see what it says.

When you see a it means it's a prayer, and a

means something to do or think about.

To solve the puzzles in Topz you will need a Good News Bible. If you don't want to turn to the Contents page of your Bible all the time, you will see we've listed all the Bible books in order on this page for you. The ones you'll be reading from in this Topz are printed in yellow. Keep your place in Topz with it, and if you want you can stick this side to a piece of card to strengthen it.

GO FOR IT!

ALL FOR YOU

Danny and his cousin Steve haven't been friends ever since Danny lost his temper ...

Danny and Steve were glad to be friends again. God, who created us and loves us, is the best Friend anyone could ever have. He never lets us down, and can help us with our lives. He wants everyone to be His friends. But there was something He had to do so that we could become His friends.

Let's take a look ...

Day 1 / The power of love

Psalm 145 v 6–13

Make a list of the powerful things in John's bedroom:

_____

_____

These things may be powerful, but what can't they do?
Join the dots to find out.

God is powerful, but He also loves us!!

Mega cool!

Join the pieces to find out more about Him.

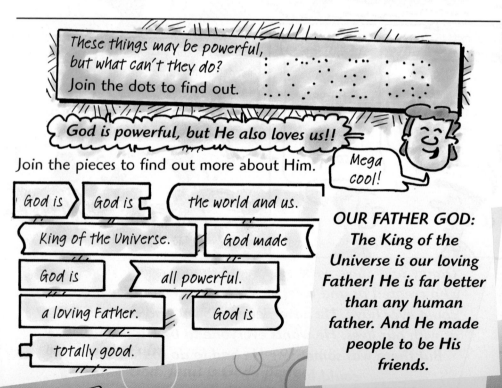

God is | God is | the world and us.

King of the Universe. | God made

God is | all powerful.

a loving Father. | God is

totally good.

OUR FATHER GOD: The King of the Universe is our loving Father! He is far better than any human father. And He made people to be His friends.

Thank you, Father God, that you want to be my Friend, and that You love me more than any other person does.

A whole in three

Can you spot three forms of WATER in the pictures above? They are all water, but they are all different. Crack the code to see if you were right.

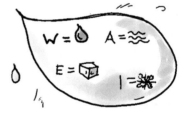

When God created the first people, why do you think in v 26 He says 'we', yet in v 27 it says 'he'? This is because there is only one God, but He has three parts. The three parts are the Father, the Son (who is called Jesus) and the Holy Spirit. Each part is a person. Trying to understand this can be too hard for even the best human brains!

Thank You, God the Father, for planning how to help us become Your friends. Thank You, Jesus, for coming to die for us. Thank You, Holy Spirit, for coming to live in us. Amen.

The Problem

Sarah is being rather selfish ...

Can I borrow your video tape of `Catman'?

OK!

Yes, but don't record over it. I haven't watched it yet.

I have to go out now, but my favourite programme is on! I'll just have to use John's tape to record it.

Everything was good when God first made people to be His friends. But people have turned away from God to live their lives without Him, and started doing selfish things. This is not doing what God wants and is called SIN.

Write some more examples of sin in this box:

LYING

CHEATING

STEALING

How do you think God feels about sin? Tick the boxes:

HAPPY

HE HATES SIN

(Answer on page 32)

SAD

SURPRISED

PLEASED

Ever since the first people sinned what has sin done?

START

S P R T D S R M O

E A A E U F O G D

Remember how sin kept Danny and his cousin apart? Well, sin would have separated people and God for ever, so that when we die we wouldn't go to be with Him, but to a terrible place called hell instead. BUT God loves us and made a plan to give us the chance to be His friends again.

We'll see that tomorrow.

Dear God, thank You that You don't want to be apart from us. Amen.

Do you need to say sorry to anyone?

Problem Solved!

Here's your tape back, but I recorded over 'Catman'!

I give up on you! I'll never trust you again!

God behaves differently! He thinks we are really special, even though we do bad things (sin). He didn't give up on us.
So, when does God love us? Tick the right answer:
1. If we do not sin. ☐   2. As long as we do something good to make up for our sins. ☐   3. Even though we sin. ☐   (Answer on page 32)

But God hates sin. Shouldn't we get punished?

God had a plan to save us from hell. Jesus, God's only Son, would come to earth to take the punishment for the sin of everyone in the world. He died on the cross, even though He never did anything wrong!

He did that, all for me? He must really love us!

Find the beginning of the chain in the centre. Write down each letter in the spaces to find out why Jesus came:

___ ___ __ ___ ____ __ ____

___ __ ____ ___ ___

> Check it out in Luke 19 v 10.

Isaiah 53 v 6 says that we were like lost sheep, but Jesus died to lead us back to God. All we have to do is be sorry for our sins, and ask Jesus to forgive us and take control of our lives.

Thank You, Lord Jesus, that I can trust You to take good care of my life, because Your death for me proved that You're my best ever Friend!

If you want to become God's friend, there's a prayer on page 10 that will help you.

He's the winner!

Matthew 16 v 21

I wish Auntie Anne was alive. I miss her.

Anne Brown
B. 1973
D. 2001
Loved by all

But, Jesus didn't stay dead!!

Who did Jesus show He was by coming back to life? Put the letters in the spaces.

What does it say in the tomb? Sort out the letters:

_ _ _ _ _

TE MYP

G O O S

_ _ N
_ F
_ _ D

Jesus reaches parts no one else can!

Check it out in John 10 v 36.

Jesus was the winner over death!

TOPZ TIMES

DEATH BEATEN BY JESUS!
READ ALL ABOUT IT!

His closest friends, the disciples, were really glad their best Friend was alive again! Fill in their faces.

After a while Jesus went back up to Heaven to be with God the Father. He is alive today so that He can be our Friend. The Father really wants us to get to know Jesus.

TOPZ TIMES

Read about the special way Jesus can be with each one of us! TOMORROW

Father God, thank You that Your plan didn't end with Jesus dying, but rising again to live for ever! Amen.

Just like Jesus

Jesus went back to heaven, but He didn't want to leave us alone.
So He sent us someone else, another Helper, just like Jesus, who can
stay with everyone who loves Jesus all over the world.

Who is this Helper? Write down the first letter of each picture to find out:

Solve this puzzle to find out why Jesus didn't just stay
on earth. Move the squares into their correct places.

Check out your answer in John 16 v 7

7 go, the	2 better for you	6 I do not
9 come to you.	8 Helper will not	5 because if
4 away,	1 It is	3 that I go

1	2	3
4	5	6
7	8	9

If Jesus had stayed on earth there would be massive crowds around
Him and we would never get near Him. The Holy Spirit
comes to live inside every
Christian!

**Thank You, Lord God, for giving us Your Holy Spirit
to help each Christian to get to know Jesus, and
to learn to live as God wants us to. Amen.**

HOW TO BECOME A FRIEND OF GOD

Read through Dave's prayer below, and think about what it means. Then, if you want to become God's friend, say it to Him. Remember that being a friend of God (a Christian) can be hard at times, but it's also the best thing in the world!

Dear Lord Jesus, thank You that You loved me enough to die for me. I know I have done wrong things, and I am really sorry for them. Please forgive me for everything, and make me Your friend. I want now to start doing what pleases You, so I give You control of my life. Thank You that You will now send me the Holy Spirit to help me live right and to know You. Amen.

Write down today's date so you can remember when you prayed this prayer:

/ /

God is really happy that you are now His friend. In fact, the Bible says that right now He and all the angels in heaven will have a great big party, just because you have become God's friend! You can be happy too! You're never going to be apart from God again! Spend a few moments thanking God that you are now His friend, and that the Holy Spirit has come into your life. From now on, talk to God every day, just like you would to any other friend, but remembering how great He is.

Here's how some Topz readers became friends of Jesus ...

I'm **Jasmine Taylor** and I'm 11 years old. When I was younger, I asked Mum about the things I heard in my Sunday School because I didn't really understand it all. I asked Dad and Mum a bit about God and I soon started to understand about the Bible and that Jesus died for me. Now I know I am a Christian because I believe in Jesus with all my heart and I know that He loves me. Sometimes, when I am worried about things, I pray about them and it's good because I know God always hears me when I pray.

My name is Daniel White. I am 9 and I live in Thames Ditton where I have lived all my life. My parents are Christians and took me to church regularly where I went to Sunday School. There I learnt about Jesus and read the Bible. At home, my mum and dad taught me what it is to be a Christian and to get to know Jesus. When I was about 4 I asked Mum if I could be a Christian and so we talked, read the Bible and I prayed asking God to come into my heart and be my friend. At that time, I was interested in knowing Jesus because of my parents but later on when I was about 6, my Nanny bought me a children's Bible and I began to read it more regularly. One of my favourite verses goes: 'Christ's love is greater than anyone can ever know, but I pray that you may be able to know that love' (Eph. 3:19 NCV). As the months passed I gradually decided that I now wanted to follow God for myself, not because of my parents.

Day 7 — Promise of power

Acts 1 v 1–5, 8–9

Before the dentist's ...

Aaagh! This tooth really hurts!

DENTIST

After ...

That's made a real difference!

When Jesus' friends were given the Holy Spirit it made a real difference! (Read Acts 2 v 1–6). When we become God's friends the Holy Spirit comes into our lives. He is a person, just like Jesus. If we allow Him, the Holy Spirit will help us in everything we do! We need His help because we can't live lives which please God without Him.

Which of the Topz Gang has the right idea? Danny ☐   Dave ☐

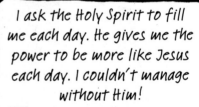

I eat 'Powerbrek' cereal every day. It gives me the power to get through the day. I couldn't manage without it!

I ask the Holy Spirit to fill me each day. He gives me the power to be more like Jesus each day. I couldn't manage without Him!

Lord Jesus, please fill me with Your Holy Spirit today, so that I will have the power to be more like You. Amen.

Make sure that, like Dave, you are connected to God's power supply!

Would you like to hold him, John?

Yeah!

I think he's going to be just like John.

He doesn't look much like me at the moment!

Asking God to be our Friend is just the start of the Christian life! There's a lot more to discover! For one thing, when we become God's friends we also become sons and daughters of our Father God. Jesus is God's perfect Son, and God wants us to grow up to be more like Him, and to get to know Him better. Let's have a look at some ways of doing that ...

Tell somebody

Jesus came into our world to tell us how to become God's friends, and He wants us to tell others too (this is what 'confess' means in verse 9). When Topz became Christians, they thought:

> But I'm scared.

> I don't know what to say.

> My friends will laugh at me.

If this is how you feel, don't worry. Start off by doing what Paul did when he first became a Christian. To find out what that was, cross out all the JKQXZPY:

I YTQOPXLD	KAQZNPOKTHPYEZR
I TOLD	ANOTHER
CHQRJIPSTIPAN	TJHAKTY ZI
CHRISTIAN	THAT I
QHKADZ	BYEPCOQME A
HAD	Become A
CHRKISPTIZAN	TZOXOJ
Chnstian	Too.

Once you've found how easy that is, you can go on to tell people who aren't God's friends. Don't be shy or afraid, but be bold like the disciples in Acts 4 v 31. Read it now. (Proclaim means to tell others.)

Ask the Holy Spirit to help you, He will fill you with the power to tell others.

Remember, there are many people who still need to hear how to become God's friends.

START

1

2 3 4

5

6

BIBLE TREA

There are many treasures in the
verses that teach us how to live, he
others trusted God no matter wh
need a Bible, a dice and

Adam and Eve created
Read Genesis 1 v 26–31 then
move forward 2 spaces

Noah and the flood
Read Genesis 7 v 1–10
Back 2

47
THWACK!

46
45
44
43
42
41

David kills Goliath
Read 1 Samuel 17 v 41–50
Forward 2

**People get
big-headed** 9

8 7

55

Read Genesis 11 v 1–9
Back 2

17

Jacob sees heaven
Read Genesis 28 v 10–17
Forward 1

Fire
Read 1

10
11
12
13

16
15
14

18
19
20

40

Strongman Samson
Read Judges 16 v 23–31
Forward 1

39
38
37
36
35
34

93 92

Abraham's faith tested
Read Genesis 22 v 1–14
Forward 2

21

Joseph in jail
Read Genesis 39 v 19–23
Back 1

The Holy Spirit come
Read Acts 2 v 1–3
Forward 3

26 25 24 23 22

27

The price of life
Jesus paid the price
that saved us. Read
Psalm 45 v 5–9, then
1 Peter 1 v 18–19

Moses crosses Red Sea
Read Exodus 14 v 21–31
Forward 2

28 29 30 31 32 33

Victory at Jerich
Read Joshua 6 v 15–
Forward 1

16

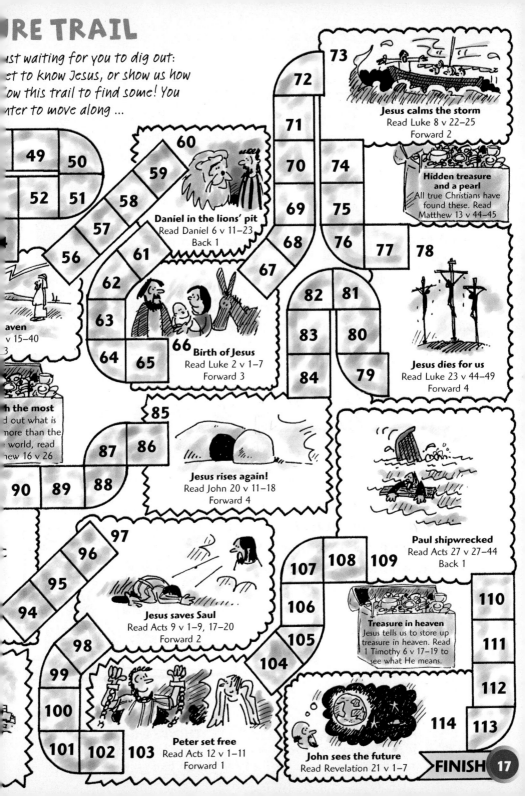

URE TRAIL

...st waiting for you to dig out:
...et to know Jesus, or show us how
...ow this trail to find some! You
...nter to move along ...

73

72

71

70

Jesus calms the storm
Read Luke 8 v 22–25
Forward 2

74

Hidden treasure and a pearl
All true Christians have found these. Read Matthew 13 v 44–45

49 **50**

60

59

52 **51**

58

57

56

61

69

75

Daniel in the lions' pit
Read Daniel 6 v 11–23
Back 1

68

76

77

78

67

62

82 **81**

Jesus dies for us
Read Luke 23 v 44–49
Forward 4

...aven
v 15–40

63

83 **80**

64 **65**

66 **Birth of Jesus**
Read Luke 2 v 1–7
Forward 3

84 **79**

...h the most
...d out what is
...more than the
...world, read
...ew 16 v 26

85

87 **86**

90 **89** **88**

Jesus rises again!
Read John 20 v 11–18
Forward 4

Paul shipwrecked
Read Acts 27 v 27–44
Back 1

97

96

95

94

98

99

100

101 **102** **103**

Jesus saves Saul
Read Acts 9 v 1–9, 17–20
Forward 2

107 **108** **109**

106

105

104

110

111

112

114 **113**

Treasure in heaven
Jesus tells us to store up treasure in heaven. Read 1 Timothy 6 v 17–19 to see what He means.

Peter set free
Read Acts 12 v 1–11
Forward 1

John sees the future
Read Revelation 21 v 1–7

FINISH

Time to pray

**Mark
1 v 35**

> Jesus prayed to His Father every day. It's best to have a special time at least once every day to talk to God.

Here are some tips:

You can kneel to show that you want to serve God ...

... Or you can shut your eyes to help you keep your mind on praying ...

... But you don't <u>have</u> to do these. Just talk to God like you would to your best friend or a loving father. The most important thing is this:

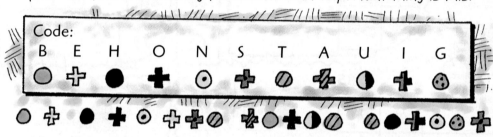

Code:

B E H O N S T A U I G

It helps to find a quiet place, if you can, and to pray out loud (but not too loud!). But at any time of day, wherever you are and whatever you're doing, you can pray to God in your head because He knows what we're thinking ...

Please, Lord, help that man to be OK.

Ask God to help you learn to pray, and to remember to pray.

THINK: When is your best time to pray? And where can you go that's quiet?

More fun with the Topz Gang!

We hope you are really enjoying Topz so far! Now that you're half way through this special edition, we'd like to give you the chance to carry on with Topz every day of the year! It's jam-packed with puzzles, fun quizzes and cartoons – all bringing the Bible to life for you. And there are great Readers' Own Club pages too!

There's a form inside the back cover for you to fill in and send off to get your Topz – a new one comes out every two months.

Or you can buy Topz from your local Christian bookshop!

Here's what Topz readers have to say about Topz ...

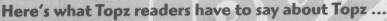

I started reading Topz for my New Year's resolution. I like the fun activities each day. The Bible readings help me to understand more about Jesus.

Charlotte Moore, Surrey

I like reading Topz because I like learning different stories from the Bible. I have been trying to learn some of the books of the Bible in order.

Emma Sneller, Surrey

I like Topz because it's brilliant. I like to draw the Topz Gang and colour them in, I think Benny is my favourite because I like his silly jokes and floppy fringe. I like the puzzles, sometimes I do them before it is the right day! It's good when the puzzles help me to remember a verse from the Bible.

Bethany Taylor, Middlesex

I read Topz because I like it and it helps me think about God. The Topz Gang are great – and they give you examples to explain things. Benny is my favourite character because he's cool!

Sam Gubb, Farnham

Topz notes are the best way I know to help me read and understand the Bible. I do them every day with my Dad.

Daniel Forester, Durham

I like Topz – it helps me to like God.

Lucy Whittle, Leicester

Talking to God

Jesus taught us, when we pray, to call God 'Our Father'. God is the Father of *all* Christians ...

Here are some other things He is:

KIND   HOLY   LOVING
GENTLE   GOOD
FORGIVING   PATIENT

Cross out these words in the wordsearch:

F O R G I V I N G
N E V E E R T O N
O K I N D O O G I
B U S T Y T O L V
I H O L Y S T E O
N T N E I T A P L

(Answers on page 32)

Dad, can you help me with my computer?

Sorry, Paul, I haven't time just now.

Our human dads can't listen to us or help us all the time.

Write out the left-over letters in the wordsearch here, to find out how God is different: _ _ _ _ _   _ _ _   _ _ _ _   _ _   _ _ _ _ _ _

(Answer on page 32)

Great! A letter from Gordon.

Dave loves to get letters from Gordon, his Australian pen pal. God loves to hear from us, His children. Tell Him how you feel, whether you're happy or sad, bored or excited. He likes to hear that you love Him, because He loves you so much.

Write your own prayer here: Our Father, _____

_____

_____

God answers

Because we are now God's children, God wants us to ask Him for anything that is important to us, or to others. Today's verse says 'the food we need', but it could be anything else that we need.

FINGERFLICKIN' TIME

How's your maths? Find and read Matthew chapter 3 + 2 + 2 =   , verse 5 + 3 + 1 =   , to verse 6 + 3 + 2 =   .

> Mum, that looks good!

> Yes, but it's off! It's passed the 'sell by' date.

DAIRY MEATS

Josie asked her mum for something that looked good, but her mum knew better! In the same way, God always knows what is best for us. So, when we pray, He doesn't always say 'yes'.

NO ← red

WAIT ← yellow

YES ← green

Colour in these traffic lights that show the three ways God does answer:

God always answers, but sometimes says 'no' because He wants to give us only <u>good</u> things, or if He has something even better in mind! And if He says 'wait', it's because His timing is always best.

Dear Father, I trust You to know best about what is good for me. Thank You for all that You do give me. Amen.

**LEARN:
Philippians 4 v 19**

**Matthew
6 v 9–10**

Benny's dad needs a plumber.

Mr Illman. Now he's got a good name, I've heard.

Illman – doesn't sound a very good name to me!

Benny's got the wrong idea! When someone is said to have a good name, it means they're known to be a good person. Verse 9 tells us that God has got a very good (holy) name, so we know that He is a very good God. It also tells us that we should 'honour' His name.

Put these words in the right order to find out what that means.
(2) Him (14) has (5) He (15) done. (9) thank (6) is (1) Praise
(10) Him (4) what (11) for (3) for (12) what (7) like (13) He
(8) and

Write it here: _____

_____

_____

FINGERFLICKIN' TIME!
Find Luke 17 v 11–19. How many of the men 'honoured' God?

_____

_____

This morning (and every morning) tell God you love Him.

Write a 'thank You' letter to God for all He's done for you, and tell Him what you like about being His child.

22

PRAYER POWER!

God really does answer prayer, and He loves it when we talk to Him. Here's what some of the children from Jubilee Church, Farnham, have to say about prayer:

You can pray when someone is hurt and ask God to make them better. You can say to God 'Do what You think is best' and He always knows what's best.

Joseph Gubb

Prayer is to thank God for all He has done.

Sarah Grasdal

I pray all the time, like when my grandad was in hospital and when my dad needed a job, and God answered my prayers. I feel relieved when I share things with God.

Hera Threlkeld

Prayer is really cool because you can talk to the Big Guy – God! You can say sorry, and ask for help when you need it.

Stephen Orman

Prayer is meeting with God. It can be any time or place and it can be loud or quiet.

Daniel Rogers

I pray in bed. Mummy and Daddy help me talk to Jesus. I tell Him I love Him lots.

Sam Grasdal

Prayer is a personal conversation with God. God always listens.

Kalon Threlkeld

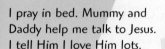

I pray to God for nice dreams.

Ellen Oakley

Prayer is about getting to know God.

Jordan Hayes

I mostly pray for forgiveness, or to make my friends and family close to God.

Drew Threlkeld

You can talk to God about anything at any time – anywhere! He loves you and will always listen.

Saying Sorry

It doesn't matter what people think, Christians

She's such a goody-goody! She never does anything wrong.

No-one will miss that pen I took today.

are <u>not</u> perfect. We try to be more like Jesus, but sin is still in our lives.

Next day ...

Sarah, you stole that pen! You shouldn't really have done that!

Yes, I'm really sorry, Miss.

Later ...

Dear God, please forgive me and help me not to steal again ...

Sarah had to say sorry to the teacher, but she also said sorry to God. Every time we sin we hurt God and we need to ask for His forgiveness. He is always ready to forgive us. But we must always forgive other people when they hurt us: read Matthew 6 v 14–15.

Fill in the missing columns to find out what Jesus said when cruel men nailed Him to the cross:

1	2	3	4	5	6	7	8	9	10	11	12	13
F	O		G			E			T		E	M,
F	A		H			!			T		E	Y
D	O		'			K	N		W			
W	H		T			T	H		Y			
A	R					O	I		G			

3	5	6	9	11
R	I	V		H
T	E	R		H
N	T		O	
A			E	
E		D	N	.

If you've done anything wrong, ask God to forgive you and ask His Holy Spirit to help you not to do it again.

The battle

Which of these describes you?

> I never do anything wrong.

> I do wrong things, but I don't care!

> I do wrong things, but I really want to be good instead.

A Christian's life is like a battle because we have to struggle and fight against some problems.

Read the soldier's shield to find our first problem:

In a battle between two kingdoms, the soldiers must do what their king says if they want to win. Do you want to be a winner? Then obey King Jesus.

Start here

Wanting to please ourselves instead of God.

Yet not what __ ___ ___ ___ ___ ___.

Jesus died for us because He wanted to obey His Father's will.

Finish off the words of Jesus' prayer from Matthew 26 v 39

TOPZ TIMES

GOOD NEWS: JESUS GIVES US THE POWER TO WIN!

Ask Jesus 'to give you power through His Spirit to be strong' (Ephesians 3 v 16) so you can do what He wants.

Remember, we don't fight on our own: 'there are many enemies, but we are never without a friend' – Jesus! (2 Corinthians 4 v 9)

25

On guard

The second problem we have to be on guard against is other people and other things. They can cause 'hard testing' (v 13), or temptation. Here are some examples ...

Put the spaces between the words in the correct places to read them:

Wemig htbetem ptedtoch eatinac ompetitionift hep rizeisso methingwel ike

Or, wemi ghtbe temptedto dosome thingwrong justbec auseever yoneelse isdo ingit.

Or, oth ersmig httea seus whenw edosome thingGod wantsusto, sowe' retemp tednot todoit.

BUT God 'will not allow you to be tested beyond your power to remain firm ... he will give you the strength to endure it, and so provide you with A WAY OUT.' (1 Corinthians 10 v 13)

Thank You, Lord, that 'in all these things we have complete victory through him who loved us!' (Romans 8 v 37).

FOLLOWING JESUS

It can be tough following Jesus, but it's the best life you could ever live! It's also tough to get to `the top'. Here are two Christians who have made it to the top, and are following Jesus:

KRISS AKABUSI

Kriss is a famous athlete and TV presenter. He has won gold medals for Britain in the 400m hurdles and 4 x 400m relay. His eyes are fixed on Jesus, not just the finishing tape or the camera! Kriss became a Christian in 1987 and says: 'I had a good time before, but I'm having a better time now. I just thank the Lord for all that He has done for me ... putting your trust in the Lord is the greatest thing in the world.'

JONATHAN EDWARDS

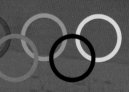

Jonathan is another sportsman who is a follower of Jesus. He became a Christian when he was about six years old. Jonathan is a world champion at the triple jump – but he says that being a Christian is more important to him than his records and medals. He has said that he doesn't pray that he will win – but that he will do his best, and not get bad-tempered if he loses! Jonathan says: 'Being a Christian is fundamental to me, and provides me with the foundation of my life.'

Matthew
6 v 13

The Dixons are the Topz Gang's enemies. As Christians we have an enemy. He's our third problem! One of his names is five letters long.

Oh, no! It's the Dixons!

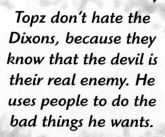

Topz don't hate the Dixons, because they know that the devil is their real enemy. He uses people to do the bad things he wants.

Can you work it out from these clues?

The first is in GOOD
And also in BAD
The second is in SANE
And not in MAD.
LOVE holds the third
But not BEHIND.
BRAIN has the fourth
And so does MIND.
The last is in ALL
But not in NONE.
(He's known as SATAN,
The EVIL ONE.)

(Answer on page 32)

FINGERFLICKIN' TIME!
Find Matthew 4 v 1–11.
Like Jesus, we must say 'no!' to what Satan wants us to do. Jesus is much more powerful than Satan, so we're on the winning side! Jesus fought Satan with Bible verses. We need to know the Bible too, then we can remember what God wants us to do.

Follow the arrows to read the warning sign:

careful, Be try he'll tempt to
to you wrong do to and
your lose in trust God.

Thank You, Lord Jesus, that You are far stronger than Satan, and that You are on my side! Amen.

LEARN: James 4 v 7, so that you can defeat Satan like Jesus did!

Shining lights

'Not hiding our light' means showing that we're a Christian. Our lives should speak about Jesus as well as our mouths. Behaving badly spoils our message. Jesus helped everyone wherever He could:

I can see!

Throw your net over the other side and you'll catch some!

Draw one way in which you can help someone else.

If we help others like Jesus did, we please our Heavenly Father like He did!

Follow the arrows to read what Galatians 6 v 10 tells us:

START

As often as we have the chance, we should do good, and especially to those who belong to our family in the faith.

Dear Heavenly Father, please help me to use every chance I have to do good, so that my light may shine for You. Amen.

29

Day 20 — All over the world

Matthew 28 v 19–20

This is Gerry and Renee Wrinkler, with their 'family' in Montego Bay, Jamaica. Gerry and Renee felt God calling them to work in Jamaica. They run a children's home where they are 'Mum and Dad' to Jamaican children who do not have a home or family of their own. The children are given a home, food, schooling, lots of love, and are also taught about God's love for them.

Jesus told His first friends, the disciples, to tell the world about Him, and they did! Many people became friends of Jesus, like them. Today there are Christians all over the world, because Christians today still go to other countries to tell them about Jesus.

To find out what the Christians who do that are called put the letters in this order:

1	2	3	4	5	6	7	8	9	10	11	12
S	A	E	I	R	O	S	S	N	M	I	I

10, 4, 7, 1, 12, 6, 9, 2, 5, 11, 3, 8

_____

PRAY

We can help! Here are some things we can do:

GIVE

£5

WRITE

Dear Lord Jesus, please help all those who are working as missionaries, and keep them safe. Amen.

Why not write to a child of a missionary from your church?

30

Run the race!

As well as having Christian
brothers and sisters all over the world, we also have
a large crowd of them in heaven!

This puzzle tells you who they are. Read every other letter:

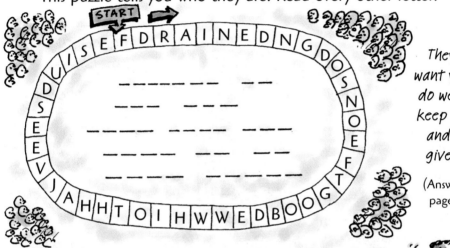

They all
want you to
do well, to
keep going
and not
give up!

(Answer on page 32)

In a race you have to run hard to win,
and in your Christian life you may have
to do many hard things, but Jesus is
waiting to give you a fantastic prize at
the end of the race! One day we'll go to
be with Him, where everything is good.

Until then, keep trusting in Jesus!

**Dear Father, help me to
keep going as a Christian
and not to give up. Amen.**

**Using your Bible and
Topz every day will help
you run the race!**

Keep this Topz somewhere safe – you may find it useful to read through it again in a few weeks' time to remind yourself of all the great things God has done for you, and to see if you're putting into practice what you've learned! If you've found these notes fun and useful, you might like to carry on reading Topz throughout the year.

Meanwhile, this picture of Danny might help you to remember four important things that will keep you growing as a Christian!

Remember – God is always there for you when you need a friend.

Love from

Lynette

I hope you've enjoyed these three weeks with Topz. But more than that, I hope you really want to keep growing closer to your special friend, Jesus.

If you have problems or don't understand something, don't be afraid to ask older Christians for help. It's also a good idea to ask them or a leader in your church about 'baptism' and 'communion'. They'll be able to tell you more.

I need all four legs or I'd fall over!

SEE YOU IN THE NEXT TOPZ!

TELLING OTHERS | FELLOWSHIP | BIBLE READING | PRAYER

 Answerz

Day 3: Sad; He hates sin
Day 4: 3. Even though we sin

Day 12: NEVER TOO BUSY TO LISTEN

```
F O R G I V I N G
N E V E E R T O N
O K I N D O O G I
B U S T Y T O L V
I H O L Y S T E O
N T N E I T A P L
```

Day 18: Devil
Day 21: Friends of God who have died and gone to be with Jesus

You Can't Play with Us, Pete!

PHASE 5

/e_e/
ea/ee/
i_e/

Level 6 – Orange

Helpful Hints for Reading at Home

The graphemes (written letters) and phonemes (units of sound) used throughout this series are aligned with Letters and Sounds. This offers a consistent approach to learning whether reading at home or in the classroom.

HERE IS A LIST OF NEW GRAPHEMES FOR THIS PHASE OF LEARNING. AN EXAMPLE OF THE PRONUNCIATION CAN BE FOUND IN BRACKETS.

Phase 5			
ay (day)	ou (out)	ie (tie)	ea (eat)
oy (boy)	ir (girl)	ue (blue)	aw (saw)
wh (when)	ph (photo)	ew (new)	oe (toe)
au (Paul)	a_e (make)	e_e (these)	i_e (like)
o_e (home)	u_e (rule)		

HERE ARE SOME WORDS WHICH YOUR CHILD MAY FIND TRICKY.

Phase 5 Tricky Words			
oh	their	people	Mr
Mrs	looked	called	asked
could			

GPC focus: /e_e/ea/e...

TOP TIPS FOR HELPING YOUR CHILD TO READ:

• Allow children time to break down unfamiliar words into units of sound and then encourage children to string these sounds together to create the word.

• Encourage your child to point out any focus phonics when they are used.

• Read through the book more than once to grow confidence.

• Ask simple questions about the text to assess understanding.

• Encourage children to use illustrations as prompts.

PHASE 5
/e_e/
ea/ee/
i_e/

This book fo...ses on the phonemes /e_e/, /ea/, /ee/ ...nd /i_e/ and is ...n orange level 6 boo... ...nd.

You Can't Play with Us, Pete!

Written by
Sophie Hibberd

Illustrated by
Kris Jones

It was lunchtime and Pete was looking for something to do and someone to play with. The problem was Pete did not have big arms.

His arms made it hard to compete in a lot of the games his pals were playing.

Pete went to the swings and sat down on the seat. The kids were reaching for the ropes and kicking their legs.

Pete reached but he could not grab the swing!
He kicked his legs hard and tried to swing.

"Oh no," said Pete as he fell back and landed in a heap on the ground. They looked over at Pete and giggled.

"You can't play with us, Pete," said Eve.
"Your arms are too little." Pete stood up and
ran away feeling sad.

As Pete shuffled around, he saw a sandpit. "My arms will not be too small for this," he said to himself.

"Hello," said Pete as he sat down. He spotted a bucket and spade resting in the sand, so he leaned down to pick them up.

It was harder than it looked, and he felt himself falling. "Stop!" squealed Zeke, looking panicked. Pete fell onto Zeke's sand fort and crushed it.

"I did not mean to fall," said Pete. Tears were streaming down his face.
"You can't play with us, Pete!" said Zeke.

Pete jumped up and ran away. He was sad.
It had always been his dream to be an athlete,
but all he did was spoil it all.

Pete saw some kids playing football on the concrete. "I do not need my arms to play this one," he said to himself.

"Can I play too?" asked Pete.
"Do you know how to play?" asked Dean.
"A little," said Pete, "but you can teach me."

Dean pointed to the goal. "You can go in there," he said.

"My arms will be too short," said Pete. "I cannot stretch or reach."

"You can leap," said Dean.
Pete went to the goal and reached his arms
as wide as he could.

The football flew to Pete. He jumped to the side. The ball shot past his arms and went into the goal.

"Oh no!" shouted Pete. "I said I could not do it."
"I am afraid you can't play with us," said Dean. "Your arms are too short."

Pete went away and felt defeated. "My arms are too short to play games," he said to himself.

Pete sat down inside to read. He was good at reading and did not need to think about the size of his arms.

He could hear an odd tapping sound coming from the sports hall, so he got up and had a look.

Steve hit the ball at Pete, he swung his arm and hit the ball back. "I did it!" shouted Pete.

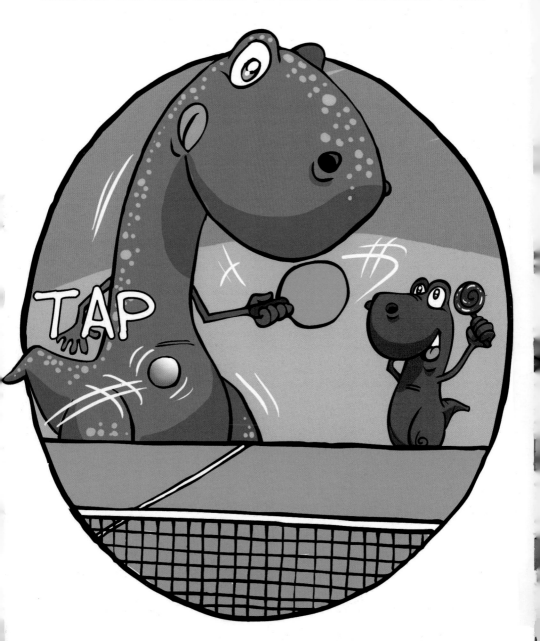

After a while, they had reached a high streak,
and Pete realised he was good at ping-pong
and it was fun to play!

A crowd had formed to see them compete.
Pete needed one more point to win. The ball
came at him and he hit it hard.

It shot past Steve... and he did it! The crowd screamed and clapped. "Well done!" they all said. Pete was lifted into the air and he felt so pleased.

You Can't Play with Us, Pete!

1.   What were Pete's arms like?

2.   What happened to Pete when he tried to play on the swing?

3.   What did Pete do to Zeke's sand fort?
    (a)   Crushed it
    (b)   Fixed it
    (c)   Licked it

4.   Why did Pete like to read?

5.   Pete had to try lots of things before he found something that he was good at. Is there something that you aren't very good at? Could you try it again?

©2021 **BookLife Publishing Ltd.**
King's Lynn, Norfolk PE30 4LS

ISBN 978-1-83927-415-2

You Can't Play With Us, Pete!
Written by Sophie Hibberd
Illustrated by Kris Jones

An Introduction to BookLife Readers...

Our Readers have been specifically created in line with the London Institute of Education's approach to book banding and are phonetically decodable and ordered to support each phase of Letters and Sounds.

Each book has been created to provide the best possible reading and learning experience. Our aim is to share our love of books with children, providing both emerging readers and prolific page-turners with beautiful books that are guaranteed to provoke interest and learning, regardless of ability.

BOOK BAND GRADED using the Institute of Education's approach to levelling.

PHONETICALLY DECODABLE supporting each phase of Letters and Sounds.

EXERCISES AND QUESTIONS to offer reinforcement and to ascertain comprehension.

BEAUTIFULLY ILLUSTRATED to inspire and provoke engagement, providing a variety of styles for the reader to enjoy whilst reading through the series.

AUTHOR INSIGHT:
SOPHIE HIBBERD

Inspired by a love of reading with a strong influence from characters like Matilda, Sophie always knew she would love to write. During her teen years Sophie explored the literary world by writing her very own novels and short stories. She then went on to self-publish these on an app where thousands have read them. Since then, Sophie went on to achieve an impressive 2:1 degree in English Literature and Creative Writing from Anglia Ruskin. Out of education, Sophie has been working for educational companies across Norfolk, and now is writing her very first set of children's books for BookLife Publishing.

PHASE 5
/e_e/
ea/ee/
i_e/

This book focuses on the phonemes /e_e/, /ea/, /ee/ and /i_e/ and is an orange level 6 book band.